STRETCH LIMOU
1928 THROUGH 2001
PHOTO ARCHIVE

WITHDRAWN

by Richard J. Conjalka

WITHDRAWN

Iconografix
Photo Archive Series

Iconografix
PO Box 446
Hudson, Wisconsin 54016 USA

Library of Congress Card Number: 2001135736

ISBN 1-58388-070-4

02 03 04 05 06 07 08 5 4 3 2 1

Printed in China

Cover and book design by Shawn Glidden

Copyediting by Suzie Helberg

COVER PHOTO: GEM Automotive Design, Inc., of Boca Raton, Florida, designed and built this Roadster limousine. Based on a 1980 to 1989 Lincoln sedan, this car was expensive, trimmed in gold and powered by a huge Lincoln V-8 motor. Notice how even the front bumpers and pipes are gold-plated, along with the "flying hood ornament." This car retailed for $85,000 in the 1980s.

BOOK PROPOSALS

Iconografix is a publishing company specializing in books for transportation enthusiasts. We publish in a number of different areas, including Automobiles, Auto Racing, Buses, Construction Equipment, Emergency Equipment, Farming Equipment, Railroads & Trucks. The Iconografix imprint is constantly growing and expanding into new subject areas.

Authors, editors, and knowledgeable enthusiasts in the field of transportation history are invited to contact the Editorial Department at Iconografix, Inc., PO Box 446, Hudson, WI 54016.

Table of Contents

DEDICATION

This book is dedicated to my mother who gave me life, to my father who encouraged me, to my brothers who aggravated me, to my wife who tolerated me and the inevitable mess that any book entails, and finally, to my friend and constant companion, Fluffy Fuzz Pooch.

ACKNOWLEDGMENTS

The photographs that appear in this book came largely from the personal collection of car buff Richard J. Conjalka. A significant number of these photos were acquired over the past fifty years from many automobile manufacturers and specialized coachbuilders, whom either exist today or have long closed their doors. Many thanks are in order to the following people who have assisted in compiling the following photographs. They are as follows:

Mr. Mike McKiernan, Cadillac Program Headquarters of GM
Mr. Gregg D. Merksamer, Automotive Journalist and Author
Mr. David P. Bennett, Professional Car Society Member
Auburn-Cord-Duesenberg Museum, Auburn, Indiana (Mr. Jon Bill, Archivist)

And, finally, to a very select few members of the Professional Car Society, whose enthusiasts keep and preserve these limousines for all to admire now and in the future.

INTRODUCTION

The birth of the stretch limousine in America was actually seen in the year 1928 in Fort Smith, Arkansas.

The coach company whose name was Armbruster, specialized in buggies, stagecoaches and horse-drawn carriages for the general public and the carriage trade. In the late 1800s and well into the early 1900s, their carriages were custom built and that was mostly their mainstay.

In 1928, they first began converting early-motorized "horseless carriages," or those "newfangled" things called automobiles, into six- and eight-door limousines. They were referred to then as "big band wagons" or buses. Their primary purpose was transporting many famous "big band" leaders and orchestras across the country to many of their musical "gigs." In nightclubs across America, this era was known as the "Big Band" or "Swing" era. Some of the big band leaders in those days were Tommy Dorsey, Glenn Miller, Benny Goodman, Guy Lombardo, and, of course, last but not least, Lawrence Welk and his Hottsie Tottsie Boys. The list of people who used these stretch coaches was many.

These early stretch limousines, or "big band buses" as they were often called, carried not only the passengers but the musical instruments and luggage, too. Placed on the roof of the vehicles, instruments and luggage were secured by tie-down hooks and rails, to which rope was used to firmly secure the cargo for long distance, cross-country trips.

Later into the 1930s and 1940s, Armbruster began producing "Airporter stretch coaches." These coaches were custom built on any automobile chassis the customer wanted and were a frequent sight at many airports across America. Mostly produced were Fords, Chevrolets, Chryslers, and Pontiacs. Every so often, but very rarely, a customer might order an "Airporter stretch limousine" on an expensive chassis, such as a Cadillac, Packard, or even a La Salle vehicle. Airport limousines were a relatively common sight, even into the late 1960s and early 1970s.

Many hotels and local sightseeing tourist groups out west used stretch "people mover" limousines as sightseeing coaches. An example of this would be the Broadmoor Hotel and Resort in Colorado Springs, Colorado. Pike's Peak in the mountains of Colorado was, and still is, a popular tourist sightseeing attraction.

Also, many special six-door and eight-door cars were produced for large universities, which often had to travel or shuttle their athletic teams to and from major sporting events overnight. This was before the advent of the van-type buses used today. Also, Hollywood movie studios used these large cars for film crews and stage personnel on their movie studio lots in southern California.

Many specialized coachbuilders, whom have since come and gone, manufactured these kinds of cars. Some of them were the National Coach Company, The Hess & Eisenhardt Company, The Kennedy Company of New York, and the American Quality Coach Company. But the most well-known was called Stageway Coaches of Cincinnati.

In 1962, the custom coachbuilding firm, Stageway Coaches, of Cincinnati, Ohio, merged with Armbruster, thus becoming Armbruster-Stageway Coachbuilders of Fort Smith, Arkansas. Still manufacturing Airporter limousines, they eventually started producing six-door funeral limousines with three rows of bench seating in 1974, on Cadillac chassis. Eventually, a product line of Lincoln limousine stretches was added, because of the upcoming popularity of Lincoln in the limousine and funeral trades. Armbruster-Stageway is credited with being the inventor and the first builder of the "true stretch limousine" in America. Moving people from place to place was the basic idea, only in larger cars. Today, Armbruster-Stageway is known as Federal Coach, having been bought out in the late 1980s. Federal Coach still carries on the fine tradition of excellence started nearly one hundred years ago in Fort Smith, Arkansas.

In 1963, the first luxury stretch limousine appeared on the "limo scene." Custom built in a garage on the north side of Chicago, Illinois, this was basically a prototype project by two enterprising gentlemen, named George Lehmann and Robert Peterson, as a joint venture. In years to come, it would prove to be very fruitful and command the respect of many limousine purchasers the world over.

George Lehmann and Robert Peterson are the founding fathers of the first luxury stretch limousine in America. By using a four-door Lincoln Continental sedan as a base vehicle to perform the conversion it would eventually become a handcrafted, one-of-a-kind, 34-inch stretch center section limousine. It was equipped with rear facing conference seating, a beverage console between the rear facing seats, black and white television, AM-FM radio, and whatever other amenities the customer ordered. A divider glass window was considered an option in those days. A price and option list was provided upon request to any potential prospect. Not many were produced over their seven-year partnership, but the one's that were manufactured, were as individual as their owners.

Even a Presidential Lincoln limousine and a Lincoln "Popemobile" were made toward the end of the decade. From 1963 to 1970, Lehmann-Peterson had an exclusive contract with the Ford Motor Company to produce these luxury vehicles. They were even promoted in the Lincoln Continental brochures of the period. They were featured in the Lincoln brochures for 1965, 1966, 1967 and 1969: all of which were available at Lincoln dealerships.

The beginning of the seventies decade showed us that many other custom coachbuilders "started to spring up." By the 1980s there were some 40 different custom body builders, half of which are no longer in existence today. Many have closed their doors due to lack of certification by the base vehicle manufacturers or lack of orders. Many have also priced themselves out of the market.

The 25 or so surviving coachbuilders today have products that stretch longer and longer as time goes on. The minimum stretch today is 6 inches and can go as long as 200 inches. These are shuttle bus-size proportions and can carry as many as 12 to 15 people, even up to 20 at times. Of course, there are also many sizes in between. These cars are referred to as "party" or "bar" cars. They are especially designed for a "night out on the town." They can also be used for many other elegant events, or even as funeral limousines.

Today's luxury stretch limos are custom-crafted on any chassis that the "end user" desires. "The sky's the limit" when deciding how to equip them and one only has to use his imagination. Many of today's stretches include the Lincoln Navigator, the Cadillac Escalade, the Hummer, many different kinds of trucks, and even the new Chrysler PT Cruiser. Also, there is the Mercury Grand Marquis, Cadillac de Ville, Lincoln Town Car, and, of course, the new Presidential limousine for the White House by Cadillac Motor Car Division of General Motors, for 2001.

The interiors and their amenities are, of course, endless in design and function. Everything from mirrored ceilings with fiber optics and hot tubs to today's wireless cellular phones are "de rigueur." The option list today at the factory, when placing an order for a limo, is almost endless. Remember, "the sky's the limit" here.

Hopefully, this book will provide limo users and non-limo users alike, insight into how the very wealthy, to the "common person" who can only afford to rent such a vehicle, may ride in style today—if only for a short while.

Read on and enjoy this remarkable segment of specialized automotive history—happy reading and motoring!

Richard J. Conjalka, September 2001.

"Way back when in 1928," Armbruster's stretch bus was the way of mass people moving or the way of moving many big bands and orchestras across the United States. This stretch was representative of the way the first stretch vehicles in the U.S. appeared. This stretch was a six-door car, parked outside of the Armbruster & Company headquarters in Fort Smith, Arkansas, ready for delivery. The chassis is a 1928 Buick which has been outfitted with a large luggage rack on the roof, along with an old fashioned trunk at the rear of the car.

Early Armbruster conversions, circa 1930

Parked here on Main Street in Fort Smith, Arkansas (circa 1930), are four 1930 Buick chassis cars, stretched into six-door passenger buses, probably destined for duty in a large company judging from the star emblems on the side doors. Armbruster & Company Coachbuilders was one of the first U.S. buggy manufacturers to convert from the horse-drawn vehicle to the more modern newfangled horseless carriage. Starting in 1928, their mainstay was large motorized buses and later, limousines. Armbruster is considered to be the pioneer of today's modern stretch limousine.

The DIESEL-POWERED AUBURN 9-PASSENGER SEDAN

An artist's rendering of a 1936 Auburn Airporter limousine is presented here for potential fleet customers. To the author's knowledge, only one was built for American Airlines. It was powered by a Cummins Diesel power plant, which measured 331 cubic inches. This was a stately nine-passenger sedan that boasted full comfort on a full 163-inch wheelbase. Its chassis and frame was designated with the model number 852. Retail price was $1,995 in 1936. It was not available to the public; designed only for fleet airport and hotel shuttle use. Notice the American Airlines emblem on the rear door and the huge roof-mounted luggage rack.

At one time, a total of 50 "sightseeing Cadillacs" were used at the Broadmoor Luxury Hotel and Resort in Colorado Springs, Colorado. Known as the "Grayline Touring Cars," these 1930s, 1940s, and 1950s fleets of limousines were at the time billed as the largest Cadillac fleets in the world. The stretched limousines on the left were 1930s V-12 and V-16 touring cars. The stretched limos on the right are 1946 and 1947 models. The Broadmoor annually photographed its fleets on their lawn. These limousines were always available for tourists who wanted to enjoy the mountain scenery and Pike's Peak, popular attractions even today.

After World War II, the Antler's Hotel and Copper Grove Resort in Colorado Springs, Colorado, ordered a fleet of 12 stretched "sightseeing limousines" for tourists. Built by the Henney Motor Coachworks of Freeport, Illinois, these 1946 luxury stretch Packard limousines were classified as part of the Custom Super Clipper Line, Series 1650 Limousines. Packard limousines conveyed tourists to the beautiful Colorado mountains and Pike's Peak.

The 1953 Cadillac Sightseeing Fleet was the last stretched "tourist limousine" made by Cadillac until Hess & Eisenhardt received an order for custom "Skyview Coaches" for the Broadmoor Luxury Hotel and Resort. Seen here parked in front of the famous western resort, these seven cars carried flags and flag staffs mounted on their front right fenders, designating them as "Broadmoors." Notice the spotlight in the hotel tower to guide cars and tourists to this remote hotel, which, at times, had heavy, foggy skies.

Here is an artist's rendering of a 1955 "Broadmoor Skyview" sightseeing Cadillac with mountain scenery in the background. This touring stretch sightseeing Caddy had it all, except for air-conditioning. Only six were built in 1955 and 1956 by Hess & Eisenhardt Coach Builders of Cincinnati, Ohio. The chauffeurs who drove these cars were always in uniform, wearing the "Skyview" caps. Notice the Plexiglas roof (there were four) panels for viewing the mountain scenery. These cars were also equipped with four rows of seating, making them sightseeing buses or limousines.

Among the most unusual Cadillacs built in 1955 were the six special "Skyview" touring coaches that were custom-built for the very posh and exclusive Broadmoor Hotel in Colorado Springs, Colorado. These were special sightseeing cars that were built on the 1955 Cadillac commercial chassis by the Hess & Eisenhardt Company of Cincinnati, Ohio. In the background you can see the Broadmoor Resort Hotel, which was founded by Spencer and Julie Penrose in the early 1900s. Notice the large windows for viewing the Rocky Mountains and Pike's Peak.

STAGEWAY CHEVROLET SPORT CRUISER 9 PASSENGER

V8 Engine 250 H.P. 9.5 to 1 Comp. Ratio 3 Speed Transmission Doors—2 left side 3 right side Tires—7.00 x 15 6 Ply Wheel Base 155" Overall Length 246.9" Width 79.9" Height 62" Weight 4500 lb. Seat Centers 33" Seat Widths 60" Head Room 36" Hip Room 66"

STAGEWAY CHEVROLET SPORT CRUISER 12 PASSENGER

V8 Engine 250 H.P. 9.5 to 1 Comp. Ratio 3 Speed Transmission Doors—2 left side 4 right side Tires—7.00 x 15 6 Ply Commercial Wheel Base 191" Overall Length 282.9" Width 79.9" Height 64" Weight 5300 lb. Seat Centers 33" Seat Widths 60" Head Room 36" Hip Room 66"

STAGEWAY CHEVROLET STATION WAGON 9 PASSENGER

V8 Engine 250 H.P. 9.5 to 1 Comp. Ratio 3 Speed Transmission Doors—2 left side 3 right side Tires—7.00 x 15 6 Ply Commercial Wheel Base 155" Overall Length 246.9" Width 79.9" Height 62.3" Weight 4800 lb. Seat Centers 33" Seat Widths 60" Head Room 36" Hip Room 66"

STAGEWAY CHEVROLET STATION WAGON 12 & 15 PASSENGER

V8 Engine 250 H.P. 9.5 to 1 Comp. Ratio 3 Speed Transmission Doors—2 left side 4 right side Tires—7.00 x 15 6 Ply Commercial Wheel Base 191" Overall Length 282.9" Width 79.9" Height 64.3" Weight 5600 lb. Seat Centers 33" Seat Widths 60" Head Room 36" Hip Room 66"

Stageway Coaches of Fort Smith, Arkansas, produced many types of different limousines on many different chassis over the years. In 1959, one of their most popular models was the economical Chevrolet Bel Air and Brookwood Station Wagon. Shown here with specifications are four different models referred to as the "Sport Cruisers." Notice the large roof racks on each of them.

Kennedy Auto Service, of Durham, North Carolina, offered conversions of Chrysler, Plymouth, Dodge, and DeSoto cars in the late 1950s and early 1960s. Shown here is a 1960 Dodge nine-passenger airport wagon/limousine. Notice the huge wooden rack on the roof. This car was a basic utilitarian vehicle with blackwall tires, and no chrome or outside mirrors. Also offered by this small builder were Chrysler 9- or 12-passenger sedan limousines.

Superior Coach of Lima, Ohio, was spurred on by the Broadmoor Resort deal to create this 1960 Pontiac Caravelle wagon/limousine for the hotel and transportation industry. Superior believed that there was a large market for a distinctive luxurious wagon/limo capable of carrying large luggage along with 9 to 12 people in comfort. The result was not as well accepted as anticipated. It's shown here parked next to a twin-engined airplane in 1960; notice the luggage on the roof.

Here, with a twin-engined plane in the background, is a Superior-Pontiac Caravelle wagon/limousine. Primarily marketed toward the livery industry this car offered 50 percent more interior space than was available in the largest wagon on the market in 1960. A center row of seats folded up against the driver's seat, providing enormous room to carry cargo. Seen in the rear window is the spare wheel and tire. This car featured the optional wood grain side treatment, available for an additional $121. Notice the luggage up above.

The 1960 Superior-Pontiac Caravelle wagon/limousine was called the "Cargo Cruiser" in 1959. This interesting car was renamed "Caravelle" in 1960. Marketed to resorts, livery services, airports, hotels, or anywhere passenger and cargo were carried together, Superior made one last attempt to sell this concept. With a wheelbase of 148 inches and an overall length of 245 inches, the Caravelle Pontiac was based on the Superior-Pontiac Professional Coach chassis. Notice the large roof luggage rack, the extra wide sightseeing windows, and the wide whitewall tires.

Superior Coaches of Lima, Ohio, offered the Caravelle in 1960, which had a suggested retail base price of $8,005. It was available with a long list of optional extras. Patterned after their commercial Pontiac coaches, this car featured a large roof rack for luggage, large rear door, and huge sightseeing window glass. Capable of seating 12, it met with little success in the hotel and shuttle area of the transportation market. This would be the last year for its production.

17

Shown here in the fall of 1960, is an interior view of National Coaches Pontiac Catalina 8-passenger funeral home limousine. Notice the two forward facing "jump seats" in the rear compartment and no partition divider between front and back. Parked here in the driveway of Vern Perry's home in Knightstown, Indiana, National Coaches cars were custom built to customer specifications but were aimed at the lower segment of the coach market; a segment that demanded stylish, dignified cars at lower prices. National also built cars on Oldsmobile and Buick chassis, but the Pontiac and Chevrolet chassis were by far the most popular.

8 PASSENGER CAR

NATIONAL COACHES, INC., KNIGHTSTOWN, INDIANA

P·60·24

This is an artist's rendering of a 1960 eight-passenger Pontiac Bonneville limousine by National Coaches of Knightstown, Indiana. Notice how the rear side doors open from the center, making them commonly referred to as "suicide doors." Because of the way the rear doors open, this car was likely a sedan-limousine-ambulance model. Doors opened this way to accommodate a stretcher patient. This car was the forerunner to today's modern "patient transfer ambulance." These types of sedan-limousine-ambulances were operated by many funeral homes across the United States during this time period.

Probably built for a funeral home in Indiana, this 1960 Chrysler New Yorker limousine was most likely made to complement a Chrysler hearse. Notice how the stretch was put into the rear door and quarter panel. Using parts and body panels from a Chrysler coupe and sedan, along with hand-made parts, this car is truly one of a kind! This has got to be the ultimate car for the Chrysler line-up in 1960. This is what National Coaches specialized in: "one-of-a-kind cars built to customer specifications." The company survived until 1973 by building many different kinds of professional cars.

The car seen here is a 1960 12-passenger, Chevrolet Bel Air conversion, by National Coaches, Inc. By far, the most inexpensive conversion for an airport limo, this limousine was equipped with a full-length luggage roof rack, blackwall tires, standard hubcaps, and an outside rear-view mirror on the driver's door only. The upholstery inside was vinyl and easy to clean just by wiping with a damp cloth. Notice the National name plate on the front left fender.

Knightstown, Indiana, had been known for fine funeral coaches, ambulances, and custom limousines since 1900, and 1961 was to be no exception. The National Custom Coach Company of Knightstown offered a complete line of professional cars built on almost any chassis and to the customers' specifications. This National Custom wagon/bus was mounted on a 1961 Cadillac Sedan de Ville chassis and featured a slightly raised roof. Capable of carrying nine adults in full comfort, it was used by many hotels, airports, and could have been used as a Funeral Director's car.

21

Seen here parked in the back yard at Mr. Vern Perry's home in Knightstown, Indiana, is this 1961 Oldsmobile Ninety-Eight Airporter eight-door limousine. Ready to shuttle 12 people in Oldsmobile luxury, this car featured all of the deluxe 1961 Oldsmobile options and trim. Notice the full-length roof rack for luggage, full whitewall tires, and the clearance lights on the roof corners. An Oldsmobile Ninety-Eight limo for airport use was rather rare! How many were made will always be a mystery as no records were ever kept. Mr. Perry was the owner and president of National Coaches in 1961.

Seen here is a 1961 Pontiac Catalina eight-door Airporter limousine by National Coaches in Knightstown, Indiana. Notice the huge, full-length roof rack, and front and rear clearance lights on the roof. Equipped with blackwall tires, this car was probably ready to do airport runs in Indianapolis, Indiana, after the photo shoot. By the way, the home in the background was Mr. Vern Perry's.

TWELVE PASSENGER CAR
NATIONAL COACHES, INC., KNIGHTSTOWN, INDIANA

C-61-27

An artist's rendering of the 12-passenger car by National Coaches, Inc., shows us that even a 1961 Chevy Impala with all of the deluxe trim could be converted into an Airporter limo coach. Starting with a base four-door sedan valued at $2,400, the conversion added another $2,500 to the price tag. The weight is added to the frame and center of the car making it around 4,800 pounds when finished. Notice the wide whites and the deluxe wheel covers. National could convert any chassis the customer supplied. How many of each model was built will always remain unknown because no records were ever kept. Mr. Vern Perry has long closed the doors of the company.

24

O-61-138-H

Again, parked here in the back yard of Mr. Vern Perry's residence is a 1961 Oldsmobile Dynamic Eighty-Eight six-door limousine, probably destined for an Indiana funeral home in Indianapolis. National Coaches continued to offer custom-built coaches and limousines on any chassis the customer preferred. This National Oldsmobile limousine is but just one example of the fine metal craftsmanship they produced. Buicks, Chevys, Pontiacs, Fords, Cadillacs, Chryslers, and many other makes were available, per request, for limousines or professional coaches.

Later Model Stretches: Lincoln

The very first Lincoln Continental stretch limousine was created in a small Chicago garage on Harlem Street in 1963. Only one prototype was constructed, and is shown here at Meig's Airport Field. These Ford executives tested the vehicle for over 40,000 miles before approval was given in February 1964 for Lehmann-Peterson and Ford Motor Company to agree on manufacturing the car. Ford executives were concerned about safety and the strength of the frame with the additional length. Production for 1963 totaled this one prototype.

By 1965, the Lincoln Continental Executive limousine by Lehmann-Peterson was becoming more fashionable and accepted in socialite circles wherever people of wealth and prestige gathered. Built now on the north side of Chicago, in a garage on North Sawyer Avenue, these one-of-a-kind custom creations were built with Ford Motor Company's full approval. Production for 1965 totaled around 75 units, and numerous government officials, business executives, and celebrities ordered them to their own custom specifications.

Designed specifically for the intimacy of face-to-face conversation, the rear compartment of the new Lehmann-Peterson Executive limousine for 1968 featured two rear-facing occasional seats which offered additional leg room for rear-seat passengers. The position of the seats provides for ease of entry and egress from the vehicle. Standard features one sees are fur mouton carpeting underfoot, a cocktail cabinet with audio/visual controls, leather seating areas, storage compartments in the armrests, and arm assist straps on the door posts.

This is a 1968 Lincoln Continental Executive limousine, one of 56 made that year by Lehmann-Peterson. Designed for people from all walks of life and occupations, this car boasted a length of 36 inches more than the overall length of the standard Lincoln Continental sedan. Available within six to eight weeks after placement of the initial order, the Lehmann–Peterson Lincoln Continental Executive limousine was priced to sell for $15,000, plus the cost of the many options chosen by the buyer.

In 1969, the Secret Service commissioned a new Lincoln Executive limousine for President Lyndon Baines Johnson from Texas. Lehmann-Peterson built this car under considerably tight secrecy for the White House. Today, it sits in the Henry Ford Museum in Greenfield, Michigan.

Shown here at the Cultural Arts Performing Center in Rolling Meadows, Illinois, is the last of the Lincoln Continental Executive limousines by Lehmann-Peterson. By this time, Moloney Coachbuilders bought most all the rights to the design and the name "Executive Limousine." The 1970 model shown here is all new and might be considered a "hybrid" as one company bought out the other. Only six were manufactured in 1970 bearing the Lehmann-Peterson nametag. In 1970, Moloney Coachbuiders would be the largest producer of this vehicle for the Ford Motor Company. Notice the custom chrome grill cap, the wide whitewall tires, and the Lincoln Continental star on the "B"-post. This car was finished in all white—surely it was a custom order.

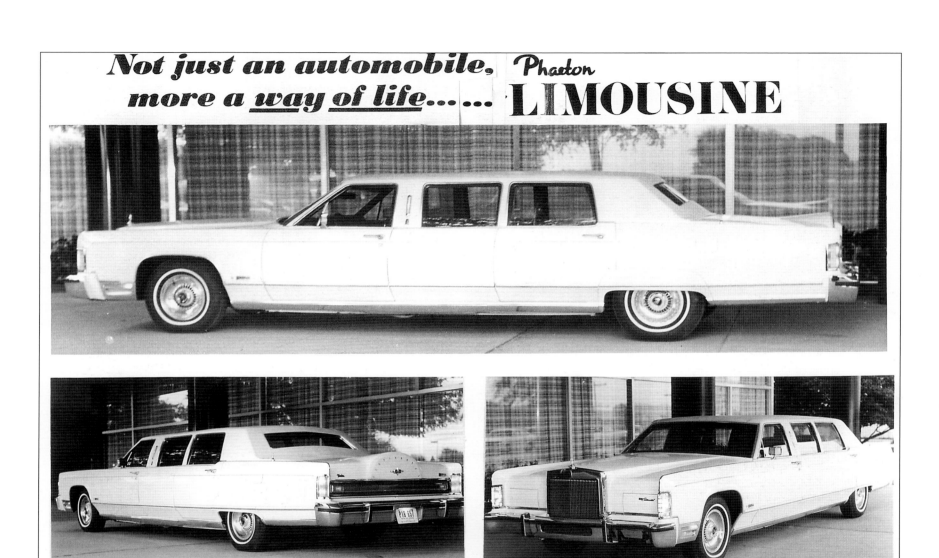

Not just an automobile, more a ***way*** *of life....... Phaeton* **LIMOUSINE**

Here are three separate views of Phaeton Coach's new 1977 Lincoln Presidential-style limousine. Phaeton Coach, located in Dallas, Texas, bought out the old Eagle Coach Company which used to manufacture limousines on many different chassis; everything from a Volkswagen Beetle up to, and including Rolls-Royces. After the "buy-out," Phaeton mainly built limousines using Lincoln chassis. Notice the fiberglass Continental deck-lid fifth wheel classic spare, the reduced rear privacy window, and the coach lamp and badging on the "B"-post.

Seen here parked curbside is a 1978 American Custom Coachworks Lincoln Town Car Presidential formal limousine. Finished in an antique color scheme of white over red, this car was a 48-inch stretch. Notice the power moon roof and interior comforts, such as television and console, as seen in the photos above. Limos like this could be ordered with almost any luxury item that was available in 1978.

Here is a 1979 Phaeton Coach Lincoln Town Car limousine made in Dallas, Texas. Texans like their cars big and this is big! Examine the interior with the center console and you will find rear-face seating with a center console housing the color television and audio controls. Notice the white phone handset for the passenger-to-driver intercom. This limousine has a three-quarter-carriage roof and has the huge 460-cubic-inch Lincoln engine.

An artist's rendering of the 1980 Lincoln Mark VI limousine by "The 'T and E' Custom Builders" of Royal Oak, Michigan, shows us that even limousines can be built on the Lincoln Mark chassis. This car was a 36-inch stretch and provided the owner with exclusive Mark luxury. Notice the Mark VI front-end vent ports on the front fenders, and oval opera windows on the rear sail panels.

The year 1984 was a good year for DaBryan Coachbuilders of Springfield, Missouri. The styling of the Lincoln Town Car was a winner, and a 48-inch stretch was even more stunning! Conservative in style, this car as a limousine boasted every conceivable creature comfort. Notice the formal three-quarter carriage roof and the aluminum wheels.

The interior of a 1984 Lincoln Town Car limousine is shown here. Built by DaBryan Coachbuilders of Springfield, Missouri, located in the Ozarks, this luxury coach interior featured it all! Just look around the interior and one can see just about every limousine amenity! Sit back with a drink and watch television on the way to your destination.

Sitting in a field of grass for a photo shoot is a 1985 Lincoln 60-inch Town Car limousine, crafted by Diamond Coachbuilders of Chicago. Diamond was a "short-lived" company on the north end of Chicago, Illinois. In the 1980s, existing for only two years, their style of cars patterned many others. Notice the interior photograph. Many of the amenities are patterned after many limos made in that period. The vis-à-vis seating, crystal decanter set, color television, and audio entertainment center were all built in the console.

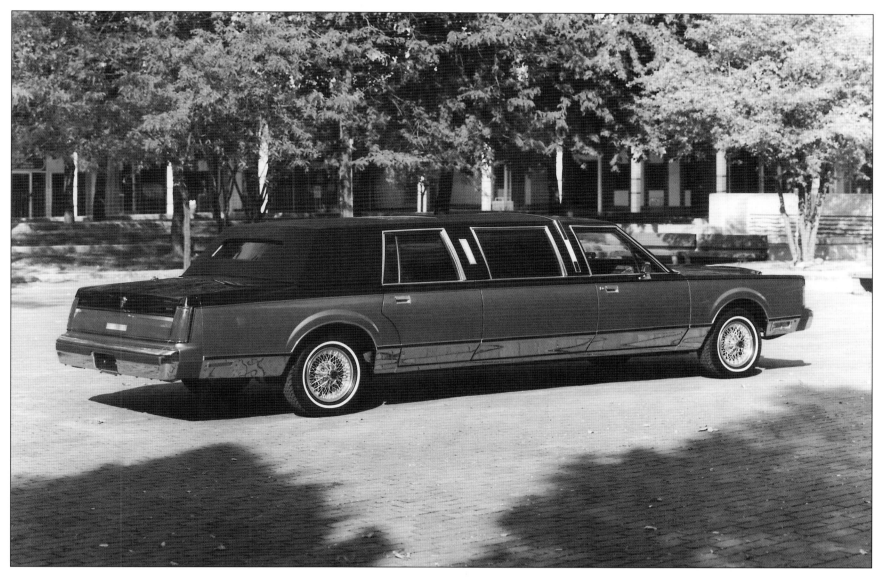

Shown is a 1986 Lincoln Presidential limousine "double-cut" model built by Executive Coachbuilders of Seymour, Missouri. Notice that the cuts are made in the center and in the rear quarter panel. The two-tone blue paint and genuine wire wheels really style this car well. The peak privacy window, as well as all rear windows, have been tinted for the utmost in privacy and luxurious executive travel! One can only imagine what's inside!

With a 36-inch center stretch, this 1986 Lincoln Mark VI limousine by Bradford Coachworks of Boca Raton, Florida, proved to be a successful limousine designed for prestigious transportation. The interior featured a rear-facing console with two jump seats facing to the rear providing conference-room styling. Not many Mark VI Lincoln limousines were produced compared to the Lincoln Town Car version of the same year.

Here is a 1987 Armbruster-Stageway Lincoln Town Car Formal Silver Hawk limousine. The Silver Hawk was the top of the model line for this coachbuilder in 1987. Equipped with full amenities, including tinted windows for full privacy, this car retailed in the high $50s. Notice the three-quarter padded top, coach lamps, wire wheels, and badging on the sail panels. This stretch was a full 60 inches.

Here is a favorite of funeral directors everywhere. It is a 1988 Armbruster-Stageway Lincoln Town Car six-door limousine. The center doors on both sides of the car were solenoid operated, to eliminate the door handles and give it a more formal appearance. Built in Fort Smith, Arkansas, with three rows of forward-facing bench seats, families were sure to be transported to the cemetery in style for the final committal of their loved ones.

The year 1991 boasted many coach builders converting Lincoln Town Cars into stretch limousines, but one of the nicest conversions was by DaBryan Coachbuilders from Springfield, Missouri. DaBryan specialized in Lincoln and Cadillac limousine conversions at the time. They also do special "one-off cars" upon request. Shown here is a 1991 Lincoln 70-inch Presidential stretch limousine in "Wedding White."

Parked in a courtyard square is this 1992 Lincoln limousine by Executive Coachbuilders of Seymour, Missouri. Notice the heavy padded vinyl three-quarter roof. Coach lamps installed and rear-quarter window deleted gives this car the utmost in rear-seat privacy. One can only wonder who it was waiting for.

Seen here in southern California is a "Mini-CEO-stretch" Lincoln limousine by American Custom Coachworks of Beverly Hills, California. Designed for a private individual who requires more room than is available in a conventional Lincoln sedan, this car offers personal privacy with just 32 more inches added in the center. Notice the small center windows and reduced rear privacy window. This is a 1993 limo known as the St. Tropaz model by American Custom Coachworks.

Parked in front of a rich Beverly Hills residence in California is the O'Gara Coachbuilders' example of the Lincoln Town Car limousine, dubbed the "Essex." This was the pinnacle of luxury motoring in 1993. Count the coach lamps on each side. Notice the three-quarter-coach roof with band over the "B"-post. One can only imagine how the inside was equipped.

Seen here in northwest Indiana, filling up at a Speedway gas station, is a 1994 Lincoln Krystal Coach limousine. This stretch is made in southern California in a city called Brea. Krystal Coaches is one of our country's largest hearse, limousine, and limousine van-type bus manufacturers, producing over 2,000 units annually!

Caught here on East 52nd Street in New York City is a short executive "CEO Stretch" Lincoln limousine built by Picasso Coachbuilders of New York. Notice where this particular car was stretched: in the center and in the rear quarter panel (8 inches in the center and 24 inches in the rear quarter panel, for a total of 32 inches). The traveling executive has the utmost rear-seat privacy behind the side blind spot. This model is a 1995 Lincoln Town Car.

American Custom Coachworks of Beverly Hills, California, presents its 1996 Lincoln Town Car limousine, dubbed the "Paris 1 Series." This is a 120-inch stretch conversion based on a Lincoln Town Car. Notice multiple coach lamps on the door and window posts, the aluminum wheels, and the heavily padded coach roof with reduced rear privacy window. Inside you'll bask in every luxury creature comfort as seen in the photo below.

A 1998 Lincoln Town Car is being stretched 22 inches and is quietly being armor-plated to Level IV specifications for a foreign government at Chicago Armor & Limousine in Elgin, Illinois, on August 17, 1998. Many limousines for many governments and wealthy individuals are "discreetly and quietly" armored. This is a "sign of the times."

These photos of a 1999 Lincoln Town Car six-door "family funeral limousine" are set in a yard of funeral coach distributors on the East Coast. Notice the middle row of seats. Federal Coach of Fort Smith, Arkansas, did a terrific job on the conversion of the original four-door sedan.

A 2001 stretch Lincoln Navigator sits in a turn-around while waiting for its passengers. A 200-inch stretch by Craftsmen Limousine Coachworks, this SUV is equipped with creature comforts that push the price tag close to $95,000. Notice the tinted windows and the truck-size wheels and tires. Here we can see inside why this stretch was so expensive! Notice the neon fiber optic lighting and neon lighted mirror ceiling.

These new 2001 models by Springfield Coachbuilders are located in Springfield, Missouri. They're known for their Lincoln, Mercury, and SUV stretch conversions. Even though SUVs are becoming more popular today, there are those who still demand the conventional luxury of the Lincoln Town Car 120-inch stretch. Equipped with luxury amenities, these cars still appeal to the majority of limousine services across the United States and Canada. Notice the many coach lamps on both of these Springfield limousines!

Shown are two interior views of the 2001 Lincoln Navigator stretches provided by Springfield Coachbuilders of Springfield, Missouri. Notice the overhead controls to adjust the climate, stereo, and mood lighting.

Sitting here "for sale" at a truck stop in Ohio, is one of the first Stageway limousines built with six doors and three rows of bench seats. It was used primarily as a family car. In its day people found out that this car was a lot more comfortable than the standard Cadillac family car with jump seats, known as the "Fleetwood 75." This is a 1975 Cadillac model.

Behind a funeral home garage in an alleyway is a 1975 Armbruster-Stageway six-door limousine on a Cadillac Fleetwood Brougham chassis. The year 1975 was the second year that Stageway was manufacturing a funeral limousine.

Here's a vintage 1978 Cadillac Sedan de Ville six-door stretch by Armbruster-Stageway of Fort Smith, Arkansas. Armbruster-Stageway was the premier builder of six-door stretches to the funeral trade at that time. Powered by a huge 425-cubic-inch engine, these limousines were not all that economical to operate. Notice the Fleetwood-style reduced rear window treatment along with the standard de Ville wheel covers.

Here is a 1978 six-door Armbruster-Stageway limousine on a Cadillac chassis, with tinted windows. Shown here in a parking lot in the Southwest, this car was ideal as a people mover (seats 9 comfortably), or as a family limousine for funeral service. Powered by Cadillac's huge 425-cubic-inch motor, it wasn't extremely economical to operate.

Seen here are two photographs of a 1979 Cadillac Fleetwood Presidential limousine by Phaeton Coach of Dallas, Texas. Notice that these cars are double-cut stretches. An additional 42 inches is added to the base Fleetwood chassis by extending the center by 30 inches and the rear quarter by 12 inches.

Notice the "window sticker" indicating that this is a new delivery. It is also equipped with wire wheels, sunroof, and chrome roof-band over the "B"-post. This vehicle saw duty in 1979 for a wealthy Texan.

American Custom Coachbuilders of Beverly Hills, California, offered in the late 1970s and well into the 1980s, a six-door Cadillac Paris funeral limousine. With three rows of bench seats, built on a Cadillac de Ville chassis, this car was a low-cost alternative to the high-priced Fleetwood models offered elsewhere. This is a 1979 model.

Custom built by Marquis Custom Coachbuilders of Canoga Falls, California, was this 60-inch stretch Cadillac Sedan de Ville for 1981. Fully equipped, including television, boomerang antenna, and unusual center window treatment, this car retailed for $54,895 F.O.B. Notice the chrome roof-band over the roof with coach lamp and standard Cadillac de Ville wheel covers.

This early 1982 Cadillac Seville "Bustleback" mini-stretch limousine was created by New York Custom Coach in Hollis, New York. An additional 30 inches of room in the center provided space for two rear-facing seats and an entertainment and beverage console, giving the executive end user 30 more inches for business or pleasure. We wonder if this car survives today?

New York Custom Coach in 1982 produced this Fleetwood Cadillac 42-inch stretch limousine with the extension in the center. Seating in the rear interior was face to face, with a beverage and entertainment console in the center. This car has a sunroof, opera coach lamps, mud flaps, wider B-pillar, and standard Cadillac wheel covers. Notice the two-tone paint job; black over silver.

The interior of the New York Custom Coach 42-inch Fleetwood limousine was none the less more opulent than any other car in its class. Notice the vis-à-vis seating and center console. The interior is done in a rich velour in a vibrant maroon color for 1982. Visible are four decanter glasses indicating there is beverage service available.

Created by Williams Motor Works of California for 1982, this 48-inch stretch Fleetwood Cadillac Brougham limousine was done in a Dove Gray with wire wheel covers. Very conservative in appearance, the wire wheel covers were optional. Notice the opera lamps on both side posts. Powered by the Cadillac 368-cubic-inch motor, it was a good performer in its day.

The year 1983 was good for Superior Coach of Lima, Ohio, a major player in the funeral coach and limousine market. Superior produced this 1983 Cadillac six-door limousine. The conversion added the center door and allowed three rows of seats. Six-door limousines were primarily built for funeral homes serving the families of the deceased. They were much easier to enter or egress from than the traditional four-door cars.

Seen here waiting for services to conclude outside of a northwest Indiana funeral home is a 1984 Eureka Cadillac six-door Fleetwood Brougham "family limousine." Eureka was a coachbuilder outside of Toronto, Canada, who, in the 1980s, specialized in hearses and limousines on every General Motors chassis. The proper model designation for this car was the Concours Brougham Limousine by Eureka Coach Ltd., of Toronto, Canada. Notice the magnetic funeral flags on the front fenders and the chrome on the "B"- and "C"-posts. Eureka was a "short lived" company due to financial difficulties.

The ultimate in Cadillac luxury in 1984 was this Executive Coachbuilders limousine. Cut in half and stretched 60 inches, this limousine was photographed at the St. Louis Airport jet runway. Executive Coachbuilders still manufactures a fine line of stretch limousines in all different lengths and models in its Seymour, Missouri, plant. This particular model was called the Cadillac Presidential limousine.

This 1984 Cadillac Limousine was special-built by the now defunct Limousine Werks Factory of Chicago, Illinois. Utilizing a Fleetwood Brougham, a center section was inserted into the base vehicle. This car was known as a formal limousine with a retail price close to $60,000. The interior featured two rear-facing companion seats and entertainment controls in the overhead console, mounted in the rear headliner.

Here is a "short-lived" coachbuilder in the early- to middle-1980s that made "just a handful" of cars. Diamond Coachbuilders of Chicago, Illinois, had this strange and unusual center window treatment with the crown roof-band. Diamond Coachbuilders would cut and stretch a Fleetwood, Lincoln, or Buick to varying lengths up to 60 inches and install two oblong quarter windows front and center. Included inside were all the usual limousine amenities. Notice the wire wheel covers and custom front grill treatment on this car. This vehicle was produced in 1984, but was billed as a 1985.

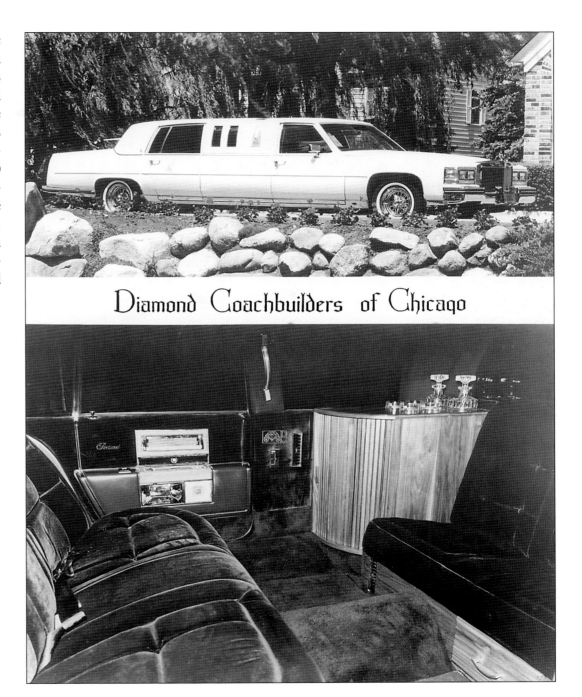

Diamond Coachbuilders of Chicago

Here is a 1986 front-wheel drive Cadillac Sedan de Ville limousine built by Moloney Coachbuilders of Bensenville, Illinois. Extended 42 inches, this front-wheel drive VIP version was not as popular as its rear-wheel drive counterpart. Sales plummeted because of the Fleetwood Brougham, which offered a lot more amenities and interior space for the same price.

Based on a 1992 Cadillac Fleetwood Brougham, this 60-inch stretch limousine was built by O'Gara Coachbuilders of Simi Valley, California. Their production was strictly limited and they also specialized in body armoring upon request. Also, notice the classic chrome grill cap and the wide whitewall tires, wire wheel covers, and "closed in" rear formal opera window on the side rear doors.

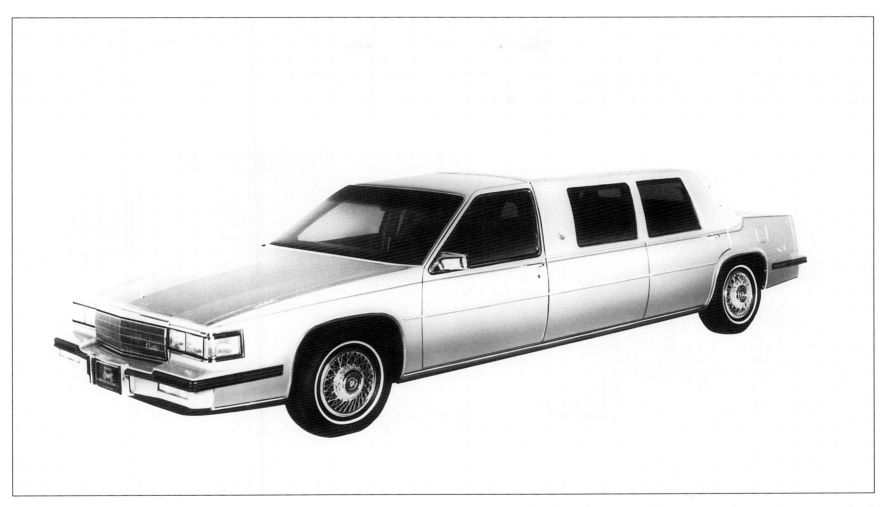

The 1986 Cadillac "C"-body front-wheel drive Silver Eagle limousine by Armbruster-Stageway, Inc., shows us that VIP transportation is available on a front-wheel drive car. Extended room has been increased by 42 inches; luxury has not been spared! Notice the wire wheels and badging on the B-post.

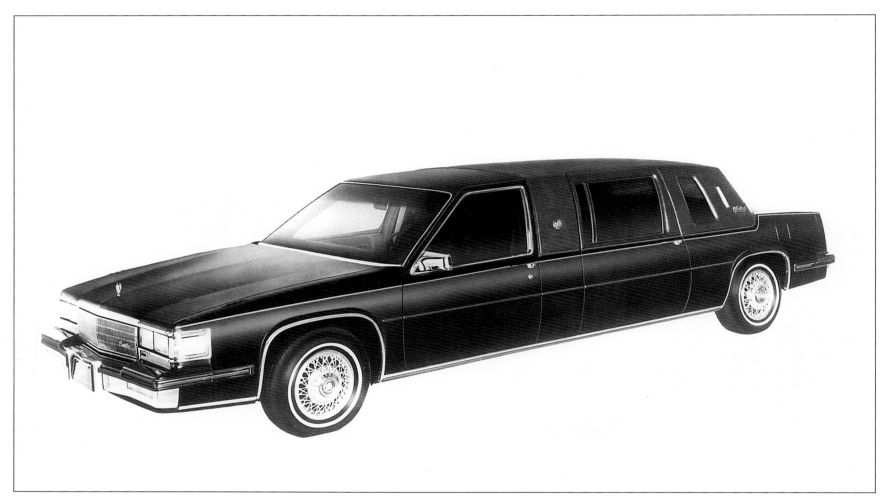

Throughout the early and middle 1980s, Armbruster-Stageway, Inc., of Fort Smith, Arkansas, produced a myriad of limousine conversions using both Cadillac and Lincoln chassis as their base vehicles. Many were built as VIP and six-door funeral vehicles. Shown here is one of the more unusual conversions. It is a 1987 Manhattan Executive limousine. It was targeted toward the executive who wanted just a bit more room in the rear compartment than the standard Cadillac Fleetwood "75" Series limousine had to offer.

A typical Cadillac six-door Fleetwood Brougham limousine shown here is often used by funeral directors for family transportation during funeral services. This is a 1987 model extended 42 inches by adding center doors and another row of bench seats, providing comfortable seating space for nine adults. It was built by Armbruster-Stageway of Fort Smith, Arkansas.

The ultimate in Stageway comfort and prestige was this 1988 Silverhawk limousine built on a Cadillac Fleetwood Brougham chassis. Notice the chrome grill cap in front, the 1942 "flying goddess" Cadillac hood ornament, the chrome stainless roof crown band over the B-pillar, the sunroof, and the chrome wire wheels. This car definitely makes a fashion statement that you have arrived!

Seen here is a 1988 Hess & Eisenhardt six-door (center solenoid operated doors) limousine owned by Windsor Limousine Services of Warwick, New York. Featuring three rows of bench seating with a "closed in" privacy top, this was Hess & Eisenhardt's top-of-the-line limousine in 1988. The Cincinnati, Ohio-based coachbuilder has been known for fine cars since 1876! Notice the wire wheels and wide whitewalls.

Parked alongside a building in an empty parking lot, the author stumbled across this 1990 Cadillac Miller-Meteor Paramount Landau Presidential limousine, with raised roof. With tinted windows and wire wheels, this car served as a six-door funeral limousine. Miller-Meteor was located in Norwalk, Ohio, in 1990, and produced a fine line of funeral hearses and limousines on Cadillac, Lincoln, and Buick chassis.

71

The year 1992 was the last year for the "square style" Cadillac Fleetwood Brougham. Using this design proved to be very popular with many coachbuilders that existed at that time. Here is one such style car, manufactured by Superior Coaches of Lima, Ohio. It is a Presidential-style raised roof, commercial glass, six-door limousine that seats nine in total comfort. The author "caught" this car parked behind a funeral home. Notice the wire wheels and custom "block out" roof with an added center section.

Seen here in Schaumburg, Illinois, home of the now defunct "Limousine Werks" factory, is this 85-inch Cadillac Fleetwood Presidential limousine stretch. Shown in this photo with interior arrangements: imagination is left up to the buyer, what interior configuration he or she wants installed in the finished product, as one can see a minimum of four are available and then some.

Viking Coachworks of Sanford, Florida, built this long wheelbase Fleetwood Brougham rear-wheel drive Cadillac limousine in 1994. The 120-inch stretch housed "J seating" with a long side console on the right side of the interior. This car was probably for a large livery service on the East Coast.

Seen here in Kingston, Ontario, Canada, during the summer of 2000 at the Professional Car Society's meet was this 1994 Sayers & Scoville Cadillac Presidential six-door limousine. Belonging to the Gordon F. Tomkins Funeral Home of Kingston, this car boasted "VIP Luxury" with very high head room, commercial glass in the doors and windshield, reduced rear privacy window, and forward-facing seats, with the center seat capable of being reversed with the "flick of a lever." Price was in the high $70s.

A Stretch Limousine in its building stages—an all-steel space frame of the Superior Cadillac six-door commercial glass limousine was seen at the Superior plant in Lima, Ohio, in February, 1994. This car is waiting for its doors and the interior to be installed as it sits at this workstation in the plant.

At the Superior plant in Lima, Ohio, is this six-door commercial glass Cadillac Fleetwood Brougham limo with special ordered 52-inch center extension as it nears completion in February of 1994. Just a few more "cosmetic touches" and it's finished.

The year 1996 marked the end of the full-size rear-wheel drive Cadillac Fleetwood Brougham. Many custom coachbuilders used this chassis with great success; one of them was Sayers & Scoville (S&S) of Lima, Ohio. Shown here along a roadside in Lima, Ohio, was this special-built presidential commercial glass, high-top limousine. Notice it has six doors, a custom high-top with oversized glass windshield, and "blocked in" rear quarter windows with a chrome band over the rear quarter roof area featuring a touch of gold accents. Retail price in 1996 on cars like this one was close to $84,000. This six-door car was the funeral director's or livery operator's ultimate family funeral limousine. Probably a 24-hour car, the center seat could be "flipped over" to create vis-à-vis seating, so people could either face forward on the center row of seats or face each other.

Here is a factory photograph of a 26-inch CEO Personal stretch for a corporate executive. Custom fashioned by Classic Limousines of Fountain Valley, California, this limousine was to be used as a rolling office. The 26-inch center stretch houses cabinets, fax, and beverage service, not to mention a portable television to check the stock market reports. Created on a 1997 Cadillac Sedan de Ville front-wheel-drive vehicle, this personal short stretch suits its owner well.

Here's an interior photo of a 1997 Cadillac 26-inch front-wheel drive de Ville personal corporate stretch. Please notice that this car is strictly set up for business duties on the road. "Downtime" for executives becomes more profitable when traveling with the office. Notice the fax machine, video player, television monitor, and lighting. For the "CEO on the go," 26 inches is just enough to house all of this in the center. *Courtesy of Classic Coachbuilders, Fountain Valley, California.*

Sayers & Scoville of Superior of Ohio, started building six-door funeral limousines in the early 1980s. The tradition of excellence continues today. These two 1998 Superior six-door, nine-passenger Cadillac Sedan de Ville family limousines were parked here for a photo session in March, 1998. Notice the Superior badging on the rear sail panels of the roof and the special vinyl tops installed as optional equipment.

Shown here in a rural setting is this Federal Coach 70-inch VIP limousine, built on a 1999 Cadillac Sedan de Ville chassis. Utilizing the 32-valve Northstar engine, this car boasted vis-à-vis seating, beverage and color television console on the left side of the rear compartment, black tuxedo vinyl roof, and many other luxury amenities. The interior was done in black leather trim and upholstery. This car was photographed by the author as it was "passing through" from Chicago, Illinois, to Ohio.

The newly restyled 2000 Sayers & Scoville six-door commercial glass limousine on a Cadillac de Ville chassis offers more than three inches of additional headroom, along with a 3 1/2-inch lower center seat, and a newly designed air flow distribution system.

Shown here in all its splendor is the newly restyled 2001 Cadillac de Ville with the 32-valve Northstar engine. It is now a 70-inch VIP limousine converted by Federal Coach of Fort Smith, Arkansas. This vehicle has vis-à-vis seating with a beverage and entertainment console among its many amenities. It retails in the middle to high $60s, depending on how it's equipped.

Seen here for an official factory photograph is a 2001 Cadillac Sedan de Ville six-door, nine-passenger limousine. Built by Federal Coach of Fort Smith, Arkansas, this vehicle is capable of transporting nine adults in total comfort. Powered by Cadillac's new 32-valve Northstar V-8 power plant, it is capable of cruising effortlessly at highway speeds.

Seen here at the 1996 Professional Car Society International meet in St. Paul, Minnesota, is a 1948 stretched Packard seven-passenger limousine. Dark blue and Briggs Coachwork-bodied, this limo has been a perennial favorite in the livery class at all Professional Car Society shows.

Shown parked for an official Chrysler Corporation photo is the prototype 1967 Imperial LeBaron limousine by Armbruster-Stageway of Fort Smith, Arkansas. The year 1967 was the first year an Imperial limousine was made domestically, since Ghia Coachbuilders of Turin, Italy, discontinued them in 1965. This was the American answer to a Chrysler division limousine. In 1967, less than ten were built and prices were between $12,000 and $15,000, depending on equipment ordered.

The prototype interior for the 1967 Armbruster-Stageway Imperial LeBaron limousine included many of the amenities one would expect in 1967. A full 36-inch stretch, it boasted fur mouton carpeting under foot, dual rear-facing conversation seating with storage compartments in the side armrests, entertainment center console, assist straps, and a glass partition divider. Not many were made; only less than 10 that year.

Parked here at curbside in Fort Smith, Arkansas, is a 1969 Chrysler Imperial LeBaron limousine by Armbruster-Stageway Coaches. With less than ten of these cars built in 1969, they were dubbed the longest production limousine in the world. Depending on options, the price was believed to be around $16,000-plus. They were very definitely "special order only."

Henry Brothers of Arkansas manufactured this 1978 Oldsmobile for funeral use. A nine-passenger Olds Ninety-Eight, it was used primarily for funeral duties. Powered by a huge Olds Rocket V-8, it saw more utilitarian duty than its cousins, the VIP models of the same era.

A 1979 Chrysler New Yorker limousine is seen here along the Expressway in Dallas, Texas. Manufactured by Phaeton Coach of Dallas, this six-door was perfect for the funeral home that preferred Chrysler equipment in its automotive fleet. With red cloth interior and all seats facing forward it was a perfect match to the white exterior color scheme. Retail price was in the high $30s.

Poised here for an official Chrysler factory photo is this 1979 Chrysler New Yorker limousine built by A.H.A. (Andy Hotton Associates) of Toronto, Canada. Parked outside the sports dome in Toronto, this car featured a formal roofline along with an extended "B"-post and center section. A full 40-inch stretch, A.H.A. tried to produce a few of these cars for the Chrysler Corporation but was unsuccessful in its attempt. The author knows of only two that exist today. Notice the wire wheels and side badging on the front left fender.

Here is a photo of a fleet of three Marquis Coachworks Special "neo-classic" limousines. Based on a Cadillac Fleetwood Brougham chassis and powered by a huge 500-cubic-inch V-8 engine, this car offered not only elegance but also power and speed. Many neo-classic features shown are the classic front end which was timeless in style, the dual-mounted spare wheels, the running boards, and the "flying goddess" hood ornament in gold. Notice the dual air-horns on the front grill, and the exhaust pipes from the sides. This car was made in limited numbers in Canoga Park, California, in the 1980s.

The Stutz Royale Head of State limousine is truly a work of automobile art. Photographed in front of a castle in Italy, every part, including the outside chrome and the interior, is crafted by hand. Thousands of man-hours went into building this one-of-a-kind stretch limo. The wheelbase is a whopping 172 inches and the engine displacement is 500 cubic inches. This limousine is truly meant for a king! It is believed that at least two exist today in Middle East countries. Price was an astounding $285,000. These cars were handcrafted at the Stutz Factories in Modena, Italy.

This car came equipped with a hydraulic throne seat to be raised or lowered through the open sunroof. Every interior feature, down to every screw, was 24-karat gold plated. Notice the throne seat, power window divider, plush velour interior, and console with dual ashtrays. Money was no object here.

Here is a 1984 Baroque limousine manufactured by Knudson Automotive of Omaha, Nebraska, and powered by a Chevrolet 305 V-8 engine. This car offered the neo-classic look of the Great Gatsby era of the Roaring Twenties. This look makes the car a classic at any age. Knudson manufactured coupes, sedans, and limousines. The company was short lived in the 1980s.

Seen parked along a river is a Crew Utility stretch limo truck based on a 1984 Chevrolet 4x4 Silverado pickup. Notice the "center section" with coach lamp on the "B"-post. No doubt, this is "roughing it in style." The builder was Executive Coaches of Seymore, Missouri.

This official factory photo shows a 1985 Mercedes-Benz 560 SEL limousine by Moloney Coachbuilders of Rolling Meadows, Illinois. Seating was vis-à-vis, with a center console in the middle for beverage and entertainment purposes. Notice the large Mercedes-Benz star on the "B"-post. Price of this special limo was a whopping $150,000 in 1985.

A 1985 Jeep Wagoneer 46-inch stretch is seen parked in a field. Perhaps the owner went hunting. Custom crafted by Tennessee Coachworks, this vehicle has four-wheel drive, tinted windows, and a roof-mounted boomerang television antenna. Equipped with wood grain siding, this was an early attempt at "off-road" luxury motoring. It was the forerunner to today's SUV limos.

Parked alongside of the Moloney Coachbuilder factory in Rolling Meadows, Illinois, was this 1987 Mercedes-Benz 600 SEL 40-inch stretch limousine. Priced at $125,000 in 1987, this was indeed a special ordered car. Notice the wide "B"-post and the Mercedes-Benz star emblem affixed to it. Moloney's mainstays were the Lincoln and Cadillac limousine lines. This was perhaps the epitome of luxury for this one-off cars' buyer.

A real Excalibur limousine attends a church wedding in White Paws, New York, in July, 1998. The Excalibur limousine was made by Excalibur Motors in Milwaukee, Wisconsin, back in 1986, and was a very limited $150,000 handcrafted motorcar. Notice the neo-classic front end for which Excaliburs are noted. Mostly produced were coupes and convertibles; limousines were built by special order only.

Parked alongside an office building in Missouri is an Executive Coachbuilders 1986 Oldsmobile Ninety-Eight Presidential 60-inch stretch VIP limousine. Finished in Midnight Blue, this car was very handsome in appearance compared to its Cadillac and Lincoln counterparts. Probably thousands of dollars less than the other makes, it still offered a high level of luxury and convenience to its end user. Notice the sunroof and rear reduced privacy window, along with its spoked wheel covers.

In 1986 the last "big" Pontiac manufactured was the Parisienne four-door sedan. Originally, the name "Parisienne" was Canadian and was assigned to the Canadian line of Pontiacs, in contrast to what Americans would refer to as the Bonneville. Shown here is a custom 1986 Parisienne Brougham Pontiac Limousine by Executive Coachbuilders of Seymour, Missouri. One can only wonder how many of these Pontiacs were converted to V.I.P bar cars. Notice the wide posts, vinyl roof, coachlamps, wire wheel covers and reduced privacy rear window.

Photographed here for an official factory photo is a 1987 Dillinger-Gaines Chevrolet Caprice nine-passenger family limousine. Mostly known on the East Coast, this limousine manufacturer did a whole series of VIP and funeral limousines. Notice the bright chrome trim on the door posts, and the wire wheels. Price was in the $40s. Exactly how many Caprice limousines were produced is unknown. Some were converted into taxicabs for use in New York City. They were known as the Brickner C-9 cabs. Dillinger-Gaines' plant was in the Bronx, New York. Their dealership was known as the "Empire-Gaines Company" in New York City.

Parked outside of a country estate is a specially extended stretch Mercedes-Benz limousine by Classic Coachworks of Fountain Valley, California. The rear door area, along with the rear quarter area, has been stretched 32 inches to make a 600 SEL limousine from a four-door sedan. One can only wonder what kind of interior features a car like this would have. It looks like it would be for a "Head of State" dignitary. This is a 1987 model Mercedes-Benz 600 SEL.

Here is a 1987 Armbruster-Stageway Buick LeSabre six-door funeral limousine conversion, equipped with three rows of bench seats. Based on the new front-wheel drive GM chassis for 1987, it was very economical to operate. The engine was a small-block V-6. Price was in the high $20s or low $30s, depending on equipment.

In 1988, Armbruster-Stageway manufactured this limousine Suburban to special order. Notice the rear roof was raised for the luggage compartment and the dual spotlights and truck clearance lights above the windshield. The end user is not known, but is most likely a large hotel chain or university. Cost was in the middle $40s.

Seen here is a 60-inch double-cut stretch limousine (12 inches in the back and 48 inches in the middle), created by New York Custom Coach of Hollis, New York. The limo is a 1988 Mercedes-Benz S-Class 600 chassis. One can expect ultimate luxury features on the inside. The car was created for Motor Van Leasing of New Jersey in 1988. The personalized plate in front reads "RGB." Notice how the rear roof sail panel has been lengthened, and the coachbuilders' tag on the front right fender.

The 1988 Excelerator neo-classic limousine conversion by New York Custom Coach of Hollis, New York, was designed to be "ageless in design" by Gregg D. Merksamer, noted author, journalist, and Professional Car Society member (who worked for New York Custom Coach at the time). The fiberglass body is wrapped around the chassis and running gear of a Lincoln Town Car chassis built from 1980 to 1989. Notice the air horns, running lights, classic spare front fender-mounted wheels, side pipes, and running boards. Equipped with coach lamps and Landau irons, this limo says, "you've arrived!"

This 1990s Chevrolet Suburban limousine conversion by Superior Coaches, of Lima, Ohio, was meant for deluxe and comfortable transportation to the airport for nine adults. Utilizing a Series 2500 chassis, this limousine was built with heavy-duty truck-like components, yet affording reliable "people moving" to and from airports and hotels. Notice the extended roof luggage rack. Powered by a Chevrolet 350LT1, it was capable of 375 horsepower.

This view of a 1995 Chevrolet Suburban by Superior Coaches of Lima, Ohio, features comfortable seating for nine. Strictly used for airports or hotel shuttles, this vehicle proved to be popular for those who wanted performance, economy, and ruggedness. The interior looks to be extremely comfortable for moving several adult passengers from points A to B. Notice the overhead comfort controls in the headliner of the second row of seats, along with the map lighting.

Manufactured by Elegante Coachworks Ltd., of St. Louis, Missouri, this neo-classic is a take-off on the Golden Spirit of the 1970s disco era. Built in the early 1980s using a Lincoln Town Car chassis and running gear, this car had the looks and the flair for a night out on the town. Notice the spare wheels on the front running boards! These designs are "timeless."

Parked here in front of a country estate in northern Illinois was this 1993 Airporter Buick Estate Roadmaster limousine. Built by Limousine Werks of Schaumburg, Illinois, it was only manufactured in 1993; this car saw very low production numbers, not more than 10 units for the year. Notice the six doors and extended vista roof.

Here is a 1993 Chevy Suburban limousine stretch by DaBryan Coachbuilders from Springfield, Missouri. Notice the mirrored center section window, as all the others are tinted dark. This was a luxury vehicle combined with truck qualities and often used by wealthy ranch owners who wanted an all-terrain vehicle along with the additional room for their crew. These vehicles were also used by large hotels, universities, and wealthy individuals as "mass people movers."

Seen parked at a steak house in northwest Indiana, was this Mercedes-Benz super-stretch luxury limousine. A 200-inch stretch by Ultra Coachworks of California, this car can be had for "in the hundreds of thousands of dollars." Photographed inside and out, one can see why. This model happens to be a 1994 Mercedes-Benz 600 SEL.

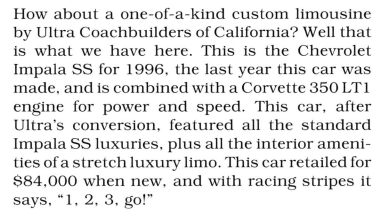

How about a one-of-a-kind custom limousine by Ultra Coachbuilders of California? Well that is what we have here. This is the Chevrolet Impala SS for 1996, the last year this car was made, and is combined with a Corvette 350 LT1 engine for power and speed. This car, after Ultra's conversion, featured all the standard Impala SS luxuries, plus all the interior amenities of a stretch luxury limo. This car retailed for $84,000 when new, and with racing stripes it says, "1, 2, 3, go!"

A 1997 Rolls-Royce Silver Spur Presidential stretch VIP limousine is seen parked on a residential street in Beverly Hills, California. Sporting a 60-inch stretch, this car was custom created by Classic Coachworks of Fountain Valley, California. The interior is all leather, with trim made of burled walnut—luxury for truly the rich!

Here is a 1997 Chrysler Concorde "family limousine hearse" built for a limousine service in Taiwan by New York Custom Coach of Hollis, New York. The rear hatch to the casket compartment came from a Ford Escort station wagon. This is definitely a one-off limousine. Cars like this are seldom seen. Notice the amount of coach lamps used and the hearse/limousine combination style from a regular Chrysler sedan.

This is a stretched 120-inch GMC Suburban being finished at Chicago Armor & Limousine in Elgin, Illinois, in August 1998. This vehicle is probably destined for hotel luxury shuttle service or airport duty. Notice how the whopping 120-inches are inserted into the base body of the truck making it into an SUV limousine with all the comforts, and then some, of a car limousine. Imagine what this Suburban will look like when finished and with all the interior amenities!

Seen on the streets of New York City is a raised roof Rolls-Royce stretch VIP limousine. A 120-inch stretch, it's built on a Silver Spur model, which is a long wheelbase sedan. Notice the chrome "B"- and "C"-posts with three coach lamps on each, and the raised roof and chrome wheel covers. One can only wonder what luxuries are inside! This is a 1999 model.

How about a big, macho Ford F350 pickup with ground effects as your personal limo? Well, Three-D Limousines from Fort Worth, Texas, can fulfill your order. Here, with this 1999 model, stretched 120 inches and totally customized, is a luxury limo/pickup with off-road capabilities, along with color television, beverage services, phone, fax machine, and all the luxury amenities. This truck/limo is definitely a one-off model.

Springfield Coachbuilders of Springfield, Missouri, in 1998 and 1999 manufactured a Mercury Grand Marquis VIP 120-inch limousine to special order only. Giving the look and luxury appeal to limousine fleet buyers who couldn't afford a Lincoln, these cars were mostly seen in the southern United States at funeral homes and limousine services. The luxury appointments inside were identical to those of the Lincoln Town Car by Springfield, but at a most reduced price. The author photographed this car at a funeral service in which the car was being leased by a funeral home from the livery company in July of 2001.

Seen here in New York City outside of Manhattan Jacob Javits Convention Center, during the New York International Auto Show in April 2001 is this 2000 Buick Park Avenue stretch limousine. This appears to be an 85-inch or 90-inch stretch. It is probably privately used by an individual rather than a livery. The coachbuilder is unknown but probably one from the East Coast of the US.

Check this out—two Lincoln Navigator limousines seen here in Times Square in November 2000. These 2000 models are 200-inch stretches. The coachbuilder is probably Springfield or Craftsmen from Missouri, who specialize in SUV conversions. Notice they both have luggage racks on their roofs.

Far less common than a Cadillac or Lincoln limousine, this Buick 2000 Park Avenue stretch limousine was photographed outside of Manhattan's Jacob Javits Convention Center while the 2001 New York International Auto Show was taking place. The coachbuilder is unknown.

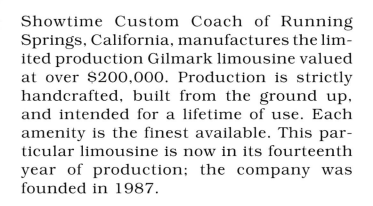

Showtime Custom Coach of Running Springs, California, manufactures the limited production Gilmark limousine valued at over $200,000. Production is strictly handcrafted, built from the ground up, and intended for a lifetime of use. Each amenity is the finest available. This particular limousine is now in its fourteenth year of production; the company was founded in 1987.

Built by Three-D Custom Coachworks of Fort Worth, Texas, is this 2000 model Ford Excursion limousine. It must have a rough time turning corners in a pinch. It is most-likely equipped with three or four television sets along with three or four beverage services. One or twenty people can really "party down" in this luxury ride!

A Hummer limo? Most definitely manufactured by Three-D Custom Coachworks of Fort Worth, Texas, this is a 120-inch stretch on the world's biggest SUV. Cost is around $250,000 for this exclusive bar car. Notice the large wheels and tires, along with the running boards. We wonder how many bars and televisions are on board this 2000 model.

Here are two photos of the 2001 Lincoln Navigator 200 stretch limousine by Craftsmen Limousine of Ozark, Missouri. These are new generation party or bar cars for nights out on the town. Capable of carrying 12 to 15 people, one can literally have a party in the rear. It is equipped with a service of three or four color televisions, audio equipment, and mirrored fiber optic ceilings with mood lighting, and powered by 300-horsepower, 32-valve V-8 engines. Handcrafted wood and fine leather appointments make them very luxurious. First-class accommodations abound!

A 2001 Ford Excursion SUV 120-inch stretch limousine is seen in an open field photographed by Craftsmen Limousine of Ozark, Missouri. Equipped as a party bar car with a fiber optic mirrored ceiling, its value is around $85,000 for the end user. Barely seen are the running boards along the side and custom-built grill. Ford recently gave all coachbuilders QVM status to build the Excursion to a maximum 120-inch stretch SUV limousine.

Craftsmen Limousine from Ozark, Missouri, produces a wide variety of SUV limousines. Their specialty in converting SUVs into limousines goes back to 1989. Seen here is a 200-inch stretch 2001 Ford Excursion limousine parked under a hotel portico. Notice the many coach lamps that are lit up, along with the long side running board. Cost is estimated at around $85,000-$125,000.

Heavily armored and ready for duty is this brand new 2001 Cadillac de Ville "protective limousine" made exclusively for the United States Secret Service. Based on the new Cadillac de Ville chassis, this limousine has been stretched 32 inches in the rear door and quarter panels, and is equipped with wide armored door posts, chrome wheels, trunk-mounted antennas, flag holders on the front fenders, flashing lights behind the front grill, and many classified security features not announced to the general public. This car is used extensively by the President, the First Lady, the First Family, and many important dignitaries across America. Scaletta-Moloney in Bedford Park, Illinois, is the exclusive coachbuilder for the United States Secret Service, the State Department, and the Defense Department.

The 2001 Presidential Cadillac de Ville seen here is wearing the American flag mounted on the right front corner and the presidential standard on the left front fender. It is accented by the presidential seals affixed to the outside of each rear door. The jet-black exterior and dark

blue cloth and leather interior are indisputably dignified liveries, among all cars. This "Limo-1" is an enormous improvement over past limousines in terms of security and workability of the inner space. This Cadillac de Ville is, indeed, an "Oval Office on wheels." Two of these special limousines have been produced so that one can be "leap-frogged" ahead to another major city or country aboard Air Force One.

126

MORE TITLES FROM ICONOGRAFIX:

*This product is sold under license from Mack Trucks, Inc. Mack is a registered Trademark of Mack Trucks, Inc. All rights reserved.

All Iconografix books are available from direct mail specialty book dealers and bookstores worldwide, or can be ordered from the publisher. For book trade and distribution information or to add your name to our mailing list and receive a **FREE CATALOG** contact:

Iconografix, PO Box 446, Hudson, Wisconsin, 54016   Telephone: (715) 381-9755, (800) 289-3504 (USA), Fax: (715) 381-9756

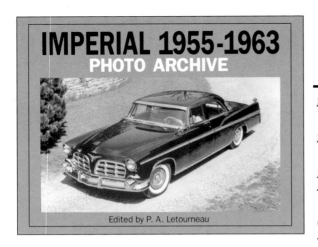
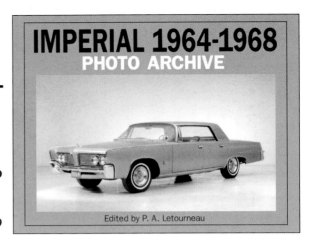
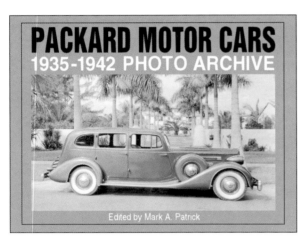
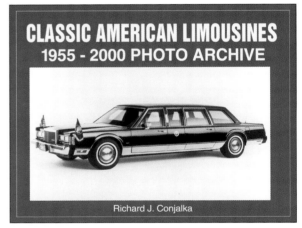
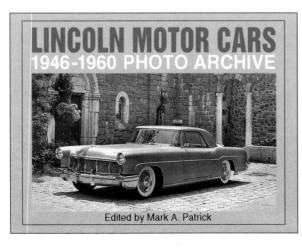
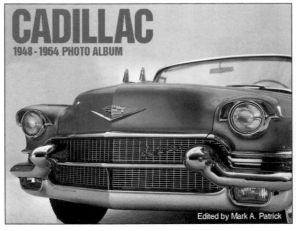
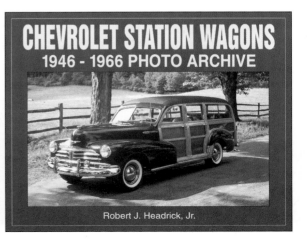